HOW TO RUN

HOW TO RUN
A DIY Guide for Romantics

.

SCOTT F. PARKER

INSIDE THE CURTAIN PRESS

PORTLAND, OREGON

MMXXV

Printed in the United States of America.

First edition, 2025.

ISBN 979-8-218-63190-1

Thanks to the following publications, where some of these pieces appeared originally: *Sport Literate* ("I Like This Poem," "Note to Self," and "WAVES," the last with assists from Sam White and Mike Gaskins); *Bozeman Magazine* ("On Being in One's Element"); *Five Fleas* ("There's Nothing Wrong"); *RaceCenter* ("On the Origins of Steve Prefontaine"); *Thin Slice of Anxiety* ("Family Reunion"); *Making Waves* ("Going Down Together"); The Joy of Running qua Running blog (several).

www.scottfparker.com

This book is dedicated to Parker Jerome and August Scott,
who remind me how to run and why.

CONTENTS

The marathon is the greatest metaphor for life,
because it's long and painful and you ask Why?
but get no answers and then you die.
—Mark Remy

How to Run

I want to say like a child and let that be the end of it. Think of how a child runs and think of why. The how is free, fluidly, spontaneously. The why is because for a child life is still alive and what is alive demands to be expressed. A child runs because it is impossible not to run. Or if not impossible, then not worth the cost of self-suppression. A child runs for fun, for the sheer joy of existence, for the sake of running itself.

What more is there to say?

Shunryū Suzuki got it when he called Zen mind "beginner's mind." Dylan got it when he said "I was so much older then, I'm younger than that now." He got it again when he said "May you stay forever young."

But, look out. Here come the adults into the conversation, the self-appointed "real runners," assuring us that running is serious business, hard work, suffering. Anyone who says it's fun or anything like fun isn't really running. Maybe they're doing something else—jogging?—but they're not *running*.

Funny how insistent these "real runners" are, isn't it? Funny how important it is for them to disassociate themselves from the rest of us, the casual, the recreational, the happy.

What about discipline, they say, and self-improvement? What about demanding excellence and putting in the necessary effort to achieve it? What about the value of hard work?

It sounds so impressive, so noble. But the child knows the difference between hard work and discipline. The child knows that hard

11

work itself is a form of play, the form of concentration and application; whereas discipline, if it means doing something you don't want to do, is the expression of a twisted mind. Even waking up at 4 a.m. for a training run can be fun if approached with the right mindset, and if so approached entirely incidental to discipline. A child lacks discipline? Good for the child.

I can be more concrete. How to run? Put on your shoes (or don't). Go outside (not inside). Commence play.

Maybe it doesn't seem like that could be it, but it just about is. Your body knows what to do if you let it. Even if it's been a while, your body remembers. Start slowly, take breaks when you need to, go fast when it feels right, and otherwise follow the path of joy. Don't think about arrival. There is nowhere to arrive. And arrival is not the point. The point is to proceed, the point is the process, the point is this way of being in the world.

To be a runner is to be someone who runs. Full stop.

But maybe you're not content to be a runner. Maybe you want to be a *good runner* or a *successful runner*. Maybe you want to run faster, to win. Say this is what you want and so you adopt a training schedule, buy fancy new shews, hire a coach. Say it goes well. You improve your personal best in the 5K. Better still, you win a 5K. You train even harder. Soon, it is undeniable: you have accomplished things; you are known for your accomplishments; you are accomplished; prizes are yours, awards, honors; somewhere some aspiring runner is looking up to you, following your career, studying your results, judging their successes relative to yours, as are you comparing yourself to those runners who are faster still. You won the race, but you didn't set the course record. You got a cash prize, but the sum was small. You made it to the trials but not onto the team. There's always someone better. You'll never be as good as you might have been, never be as good as you could be. You are, in other words, doomed to feeling like a failure. Sorry.

Or don't run. Who cares? No one cares. No one besides you. Your spouse doesn't even care. Be a good spouse, a good parent, a good friend. People care about that. No one cares if you run. Unless.

Unless they can see that running is good for you. They care about you and your doing things that are good for you. If running is good for you, run! they will say. If running brings you rewards you can't get elsewhere, run. If it brings you joy or meaning or peace, do it. If it helps you to feel like yourself, just do it. Don't do it because you're good at it. Do it because you love it.

Did you ever stop a running child to ask them why they were running? No, you did not. We tend to be silenced in the face of true beauty, and everyone sees that a running child is a moving beauty. Don't you know this. Haven't you always. Isn't there still a child inside you. Isn't that child right now telling you in no uncertain terms: *let's go.*

I Like This Poem

I get it. It's not like those ones in school
where the teacher asks if you can identify
all the metaphors for God or democracy
or whatever. What is a metaphor anyway?

And why can't a poem just be about
whatever it's about, like this one,
which is about running. I get running.
Everyone knows what running is.

So when the poet says running
we all know what he's talking about
and we know that it just means running
and not some other thing about mortality

or the will to power or anything
hifalutin like that. Running is running.
That's it. And there's no reason on Earth
to make it any more complicated than that.

Note to Self

Just to help you remember
that in the summer you were forty-one
and your older boy—
the one you didn't know you'd have
never mind love
more deeply than the ocean
—was five
you were at the beach in Oregon
and you were running, the two of you,
with your feet in the water, splashing
for minutes hours miles—how many miles—
how many thousands of infinities.

You'd run this way a hundred times before
alone but never with your boy
who never got tired as the sun never set
and the waves kept coming
washing up ankles to knees
and you swooped like birds in the break
and if there were some separation
between the two of you
what was it and where and when?
They say there are no gaps in nature
and you could not find any.

So if one day you are too old to run, remember
or if you don't ever make it back to the beach
or if your son, when he's a certain age,
wants nothing to do with you, remember
that whatever else happens
this summer happened too.

On Being in One's Element

My whole life, I've been on a first-name basis with the rain. I know it intimately and directly, like gravity or my own breath, and therefore trust it. It is the only element I inhabit without hesitation or self-consciousness. It is, in fact, very often what I mean when I use the word *home*.

Snow, by contrast, is still a stranger to me, even as I've been in the frigid north since leaving Portland in 2009. On any given winter—not to mention spring—morning I may be found staring out the window once again in disbelief that the snow has stuck around another day. I do not deny the stark beauty of it, nor the recreational opportunities it affords. But while I may appreciate them, these are not my beauties or my opportunities. My loyalties remain with the rain.

But there's only so long you can nod at a stranger before you introduce yourself. I decided this December, not for the first time, to approach the winter and find out if we might be friends. This is maybe a long way of saying that I went for a run the other day, but the run itself was a long time coming.

When I accepted the assignment to write this article, the winter and I didn't get off to the warmest start. No sooner had I put on my dorky spandex running pants and rummaged through a box in the garage until I found the ice cleats my university had issued me a few winters ago and that sort of fit over my shoes than my wife, Sandy, asked me how cold it was outside. I told her I didn't know and wondered why it mattered. According to the internet, she told me, it wouldn't be good for my lungs to run when the temperature was below fifteen. Rest assured, that nothing good ever comes of Sandy reading articles on the internet. We checked the temperature. It was ten degrees with a windchill of six. She asked me to wait until it was warmer—my asthma and so on—ideally after Christmas, when I might be on the receiving end of a pair of warm gloves. But *Bozeman Magazine*'s Angie Ripple doesn't have time to wait for warm gloves. There was a job to be done. I told Sandy I could wait for warmer weather but that my deadline was looming.

On the brink of that deadline, with the temperature approaching twenty, I put on two pairs of lightweight running gloves, along with the rest of my hodgepodge of inadequate gear, and drove over to Sourdough, where I opened the car door to be confronted with clouds of smoke like I had somehow woken up from the dream of winter to find myself smack in the middle of September.

Nevertheless, there I was, and off I went. Half a mile in, the smoke growing thicker, me growing less and less sure of this excursion, I came to the source: a smoldering slash pile of debris like a small volcano, where the logs from last fall's thinning of the forest had been stacked, an eerie juxtaposition of fire and ice I observed from the relief of the windward side. As I left the burn behind, the air quickly cleared, and I thought maybe the run I was hoping for was about to begin.

I fully admit to being the kind of runner who romanticizes the sport, at least when it is practiced outdoors, where you can find me communing with nature, confronting the sublime, or struggling heroically against my limits—you name it, and I'll be there trying to have a moment.

Which was a lot of pressure to put on trudging up a hill in the snow flexing my hurting cold fingers. Sometimes even I must admit that a run is just a run and that the gym-goers of the world at least have the advantage of full feeling in their extremities. Thinking such thoughts, I might even have turned around and waited for May. But, like I said, there was a job to be done. For the sake of journalism, I continued.

I'm sure you know what it was like up there. Snow and more snow, skiers and their dogs, the clouds of my exhales dissipating before my eyes, all sound absorbed into the muffling covering of accumulated snow. Nothing to sneeze at, but nothing either that I needed to stick around for when I could just jot down a few impressions and beat a downhill retreat to the warm car.

But when I got up a couple miles and the trail started opening up over the creek and the sunlight was shining through the treetops with increasing regularity, I figured I'd go a little farther. Pretty soon, the trail started to flatten out, the fact that I'd barely run since my marathon two months ago started to feel insignificant, and I picked up my pace ever so slightly. The skiers I was passing on the way up would pass me on the way down, but so what; right now I was feeling pretty good. It wasn't cold running or winter running or snow running, it was just running, the same kind of running I've been doing for a quarter century. My body knew what to do, and I was remembering why I do it and why I love nothing more.

I knew I could go on a long way like this, watching the sunlight sparkle through a flurry of snow whenever a gust of wind announced itself. Sometimes a run gets easier the farther into it you go. This was turning into one of those runs. Eventually there came the tug of responsibility—papers to grade, children to care for, this article to write—but for a while there I felt it: the temptation to run forever into the snowy mountains and run myself toward an exhaustion that would never come.

The way down was fast and easy. I felt fine, like it was nothing out of the ordinary, this running in the snow. But the closer I came to the car, the less inspired it felt. Whatever I was approaching up there before the turnaround was still up there. It hadn't followed me down. It rarely does. And those things we leave behind when we go into the woods—responsibilities, stress, noise, and all the rest—they're there waiting for us when we return.

I haven't succeeded yet in making friends with the snow, but give me time; it's only been thirteen years since I left the rain. Never mind that, though. I don't need to be at home in the snow. I need only to be respectful of it. To adjust to the temperature, to get a pair of warm gloves, to interact with the world as I find it, to let it take me to the same places the rain always has: that place that is always just a little farther down the trail, that like Zeno we can approach indefinitely but never—thankfully, *thankfully*—arrive at.

On the Origins of Steve Prefontaine

Forty-five years after his untimely death, Steve Prefontaine's hold on the running world's imagination is still unrivaled. Already the subject of three feature films—two Hollywood biopics as well as the documentary *Fire on the Track*—Pre appears now in a fourth, *Pre's People*. This documentary, directed by Travis Johnson, alumnus of both Coos Bay's Marshfield High School and the University of Oregon, breaks from the mytho-biographical mould established by the earlier films, foregrounding instead the context in which Pre's heroic and tragic story was set.

The great success of *Pre's People* is that, by turning its camera from Pre and inviting us to see him through the eyes of the people who knew him, it allows Pre to resolve into a depth and clarity that hasn't previously been achieved in film. This Pre is more sensitive, less brash than fans have come to expect—less heroic, more human.

Take, for example, two of Pre's high school races. First, climactically, his attempt to set the national 2-mile record. Knowing his success in advance does not damper the joyous intensity of reliving the race in oral-history fashion. Here is Pre as conquering hero. By poignant contrast, his subsequent failed attempt to break four minutes in the mile reveals Pre's vulnerability. According to Ron Apling, one of Pre's Marshfield teammates, Pre's post-race dejection wasn't on his own behalf but on that of his hometown crowd. "They had all come to watch him and he hadn't done what he wanted to do for 'em."

For those of us who grew up steeped in the mythology of Prefontaine, whether in Oregon or elsewhere, there is much to be gained by such doses of reality. They keep us honest and puncture the hagiography that often attends Pre's legacy. As Bob Welch puts it, "I think sometimes people try to make Pre more than he actually was. He was just a great runner who gave it his all. And that's enough. I don't think that we need to make him into a god." Nevertheless—or, perhaps, *therefore*—the myth withstands. Pre's example, after all, has always been one of dedication and courage—mortal virtues if ever there were.

Such is the portrait that emerges from the testimonials of former coaches, former teammates, former rivals, and lifelong fans: a hardworking kid who had more in common than not with the other hardworking kids of Coos Bay. These testimonials, which are as affectionate as they are proud, coupled with historical and geographical surveys of Coos Bay, bring Pre back home. We're glad to share him with the world, *Pre's People* declares, but in the end he's ours.

One of the most endearing statements in the film comes from Jared Bassett, a former Marshfield runner, who says, "Sometimes running out in the dunes you kinda just feel like he's out there still, training with you almost. It's a neat feeling." It's one of those things about Pre that the more you know about him the closer to him you inevitably feel.

But from the felt sense that he's still alive to the lingering shock that he isn't, Brad Jenkins, Johnson's co-executive producer on the film, who also grew up and ran competitively in Coos Bay, recalls, "Travis and I were just eleven years old when we both saw Pre set his last American record, which happened to be on Marshfield's track . . . the 2,000m in 5:01.4 set in 1975. A few weeks later, we were on that same track at his funeral."

That sequence of events, needless to say, has stayed with Jenkins and Johnson. In 2011, realizing how much local Prefontaine lore had gone undocumented, they began what became the ten-year process of conducting interviews and acquiring old footage and photographs. It has been a labor of love for these lifelong friends, the product of which is a gift for all of us who continue to draw meaning from the life and example of Pre. Who are his people? We are.

On Not Being Kipchoge

Note to the runners out there: Take heart. Even Kipchoge is not Kipchoge. He was Kipchoge once, but now he is Kipchoge. You see what I mean? It is a lifelong project to be who you are—a project perpetually begun yet always complete. Such is the mysterious logic to which being adheres. Not being Kipchoge is a gift to all who are not Kipchoge. Not being Kipchoge is no reason not to not be Kipchoge. Only Kipchoge runs to be Kipchoge, which he does simply by running. It is the same for us as it is for him, each of us running only to be who we are running. And since we are the same, each of us who we are, we therefore are one, therefore are Kipchoge, all of us.

Dumb Runner

for Mark Remy

Tired of thinking, tired of thought, let me run dumb.

Unthinkingly. Stupidly. Bodily. Physically. Naturally. Instinctually.

Like a lion is chasing me or the path by the sea is home ground to my flexed foot and the sun is making promises it will keep.

My bones know things my mind never will. The language my muscles speak is the truth.

If on the far side of exhaustion lies silence and on the near, possibility, I want to run right up to the line and keep myself there, an apprentice to the erotics of the run.

Desire, then, to be admitted to the elemental and to have nothing more to say.

Runner as Solipsist
A Rant

Runners are regularly subject to a slew of insults, "solipsistic" not least among. It, like many terms of disparagement, is the result of fear. A runner's self-contained disposition looks like self-worship to someone who lacks it. The presumed vanity that explains the regular pursuit of solitude. There's something suspicious about a person who doesn't need to be constantly distracted from their own interiority. What is wrong with them? If they aren't stupid, they must be solipsists.

I see what these critics mean. We are unusually attuned to our private well-being. We run as much as we do because it is our most reliable source of meaning and joy, the most honest expression of who we are. But on further reflection, I would hardly call this kind of self-awareness solipsistic. On the contrary, we have the perspective to observe that running is our preferred way of being in the world.

Therefore, solipsism is a charge against which I will eagerly defend most runners most of the time. But, my god, you people, do me a favor and take the damn earbuds out of your head holes. When you can't hear the person coming from behind to pass you on the single-track trail, never mind the music of the wind through the tall grass, you aren't running outside; you're attempting to make the outside the inside, which is the definitional ambition of the solipsist.

If you want to live and run in a private bubble carefully curated by you and your favorite algorithms, the apparatus of the entire consumer world is posed to assist you. But if you want to live in that private bubble, have the common courtesy to keep it private. Don't let your closed-off reality crash into our shared one.

Or, better yet, don't isolate yourself in a private space of your own design in the first place. Don't forget that the appeal of running is that it opposes that very impulse. It puts you in the world, where, like your ancestors and your fellow homo sapiens, you belong.

Turn down the interference and you will hear what the subtler parts of yourself are already telling you: the world is enough.

Run there.

A Few Notes on Racing

No sooner is the gun raised than it is fired. Chekhov would approve.

The calmest place to be during a race is running it.

For some reason, there are people who will spend their leisure time watching you race. Those GO RANDOM STRANGER signs? They're for you.

The paradox at the heart of racing is that the point of this activity we profess to love is for it to be over as quickly as possible. The point of running a race is to get it over with.

Philosophers would call this the difference between telic and atelic goals. The more time we spend doing what we love, the more we have failed. We run toward what we want but not through it. The end justifies the means. Or fails to. We race so that we can have raced. The present self submits to the future self.

There is no limit to the number of times you can achieve a personal record, but as soon as you stop getting faster you start getting slower.

You cannot know your best until it's behind you.

Which mostly it is.

Obscenities in Paradise
Another Rant (Nearly)

With a good hour to kill before the start of the Bozeman Half Marathon, I perched myself atop a fence post to watch the Rocky Mountain sunrise. I hoped to run fast this morning, and with a pink sky looming over the Bridgers anything seemed possible.

Other runners passing time before the start of the race paced or jogged past my perch. Some of them I regarded, others I ignored, as my idle mind drifted this way and that. There is a certain stillness that is available only in the moments before intense action. When the race started, I'd be running. For the time being, I was right there doing nothing in particular.

It sounds idyllic, does it not? It was. Mountains, skies, human bodies preparing for exertion—it was an elemental morning.

Except, when I studied the runners moving by my fence post I saw that a great many of them were wearing what I could tell were the carbon-plated supershoes that had so disrupted our simple sport over the preceding few years. And these runners did not belong to, shall we say, the sport's elite. They were my middle age or older, they were stiff, they were heavy. Most of them, I estimated, would be lucky to break two hours. Despite all this, they wore the shoes of Olympians.

What possesses noncompetitive runners to spend hundreds of dollars on shoes that may marginally improve their times? And what possesses me, a runner who on a good day can still place in his division, to resist?

For me, it's surely in part a combination of pride, personality, and my allegiance to an antiquated distinction between *natural* and *artificial*. But more than any of these, it's plain old self-consciousness. I wouldn't want to be seen as the kind of person who would wear high-tech elite racing shoes while churning out seven-minute miles. It would be embarrassing.

But these runners had, to my eye, lost the capacity for embarrassment. These were the kind of people who might ask me sincerely why in a world with fast shoes they should run in slow shoes. What could I say to them? How could I try again to explain that the point is the running itself, not the times that can be engineered by the mad scientists at Nike?

I didn't know what to feel. Part of me wanted to laugh at these ridiculous creatures made doubly ridiculous for the fact they couldn't see how ridiculous they were in the first place. Another part of me wanted to curse how fake accomplishments cheapen real ones. A third part of me inclined toward pity: What kind of emotional depravity must a person know to be susceptible to the ad campaigns of Nike? Who thinks that if they can shop their way from a 2:08 half to 2:05 they'll deserve their own personal Wheaties box?

Supershoes neither stand for nor encourage athletic excellence. They stand for and invite only entitlement. You can spend your way to a time that five years ago you would have had to work for. It is once again a way for wealth to tilt the even ground. How could a sane person not rant that these shoes represent everything that's wrong with our results-focused and number-obsessed sport? Who could argue that in its granting of unearned benefits it's any different from doping?

But here's the thing about running: the self-righteousness, the offended sensibility, the inner diatribe—you can leave them all behind simply by moving your legs. When the race started, I ran. And because I didn't look back, my problems were all behind me.

Ahead of me, the sky was still pink, I was back in paradise.

Elevation Change

I was running fine last summer in Bozeman, maybe even well. But not by a mile was I expecting to wake up one morning to find I'd been incarnated as a better runner than I'd ever hoped to become. And yet.

Early on my first morning visiting my parents in Oregon, I laced up my shoes and jogged down to the path along the river. We were expecting heat later in the day, but conditions were ideal at sunrise. With the trees looming above me, the river sparkling below me, and the air filling my lungs with the rich oxygen of home, I took to the path like any animal returned to its native habitat.

There are days—any runner knows them—when we surprise ourselves. This, for me, was one of those days. It was as if my legs had been removed in the night and replaced by the legs of a superior runner. It wasn't the speed itself that enthralled me. It was the ease of the speed. The farther into the run I got the faster I went. Yet no matter how fast I went I never could feel like I was straining. I wasn't quite foolish enough to think I was without limits, but it sure felt to me exactly as if I were without limits.

But if my body was not my own, my thoughts mostly were. I recognized myself in my mind. If I had undergone a metamorphosis in the night, I thought, would I of all people be the one to know it? Yet was this awareness itself not evidence enough that I was still me enough to notice that I wasn't? It gets metaphysical quickly, this running.

Maybe I should stop thinking, I thought, and simply enjoy what had to be due simply to the elevation change between the Gallatin and Willamette valleys. I had long wanted to be the kind of person who is graceful enough to accept life's gifts when they are given.

And so I ran as only this particular animal on this particular day could. What choice was there? If a runner knows anything, he knows this.

Later, back at my parents' place, I reflected that whatever mystery had produced this run and elevated me, however briefly, into a different class of runner was the same mystery that assigned me the ability I usually knew myself to possess. The fact of an easy seven-minute pace is every bit the miracle of the six-minute pace.

I went out again the next morning. I ran fine, maybe even well. But I was the same old me again, as I reasoned I had been all along, even if for a single morning I felt like I was someone else entirely.

Phenomenology of Running

Pay close enough attention to running and it ceases to be "running." Legs, too, cease to be "legs." Ditto: breathing and "breathing"; body and "body"; experience and "experience." Running, like anything, is inscrutable but from a distance. To scrutinize is to apply language, to chunk experience, to impose stases on dynamic processes. That is, it takes us from running to "running," from experience to concept. But while some cases clearly are running and some cases clearly are not, there are gray areas on the edges of the concept that have no bearing on experience as such. Is that "running" or is it "jogging"? Is that "running" or is that "playing"? Is that "running" or is that "actively not falling down"? Call it what you want to, the ground beneath the runner's feet is the ground of experience. And what's happening doesn't feel like anything, it just feels.

Time to No Thing

1) No things but in time.

2) I-no-I running yesterday-no-yesterday up the mountain-no-mountain through the trees-no-trees for an hour-no-hour until I-no-I seeing the view-no-view: city-no-city land-no-land things-no-things matter-no-matter.

3) Running breathing running thinking running quieting running ascending running turning running cresting running descending running grounding running treeing running rocking running mountaining running birding running squirreling running deering running winding running watering running sunning running birthing running dying running disappearing running changing running beginning running timing running stopping running resuming running.

"Sneakers"

When my sister and I were kids, we had friends who lived on the next block. One day they came home with a cassette tape they wanted to play for us. When I heard the opening song, "Sneakers," I felt like it had been made just for me.

Maybe we all felt that way. That spring, we played "Sneakers" every day as we ran laps around their foyer, boombox in the center of our track blasting out lyrics I'll never forget:

When I run, I run, I run, I really flyyyyyyyyyy

When the song ended, we caught our breaths as the tape rewound. Then we hit play again on what was effectively another track repeat. Whole afternoons passed this way.

How old was I that year? Maybe seven. And how many more years would it be until I relearned what I knew then? That the body is where joy lives. That fun is a renewable resource. That art can be at once fully personal and fully communal.

I don't know if the neighbor kids ever took up running again the way we did as kids. I don't know if those afternoons meant to them what they meant to me. We lost touch years ago. But this year for Christmas my sister gave me a vinyl record by a band whose name I didn't recognize: The Tickle Tune Typhoon. Curious, I put it on the turntable. A few new notes into the first song I was clearing space in the hallway and telling my son to get ready. It was time for us to fly.

First to Last

The pleasure of watching sports is rarely about the outcome and almost always about preparing yourself to appreciate moments of poignancy when they occur as they will without warning.

I was reminded of this and of track's abiding virtue at a recent dual meet at the local high school. The winning runner in the girls 1,500m had crossed the line in about 5:40. I had clapped encouragingly alongside my wife and son and most of the fans in the sparsely populated bleachers. Some of the runner's friends and classmates had called out her name as they cheered. Good for her. But as the second and third runners finished the stadium had returned to murmuring conversation punctuated by a regular and respectful applause for the trailing runners as they came across over the next minute or two.

It could have gone on winding down this way until the next race began, except that for anyone paying attention to the whole field there was still one runner with a full lap to go. She was so far behind it was as if she were in a different race. And, really, she might have been for all the chance she had to move up to even second from the back.

The real competition in track, you will sometimes hear, isn't the field but the clock. But as pure as that claim may sound it's still one step removed from the truth. You don't need a clock. Your competition in track is yourself. Not your abstract self or your best-ever self but your actual self on a given day. The test of a race is whether you can rise to the challenge of performing the best possible version of yourself in that moment. Your effort must be your best—but best is always relative.

There was no pity in my tears for the last-place runner as she rounded the final curve. Because I have rounded a hundred final curves myself, because among the days when I have not done my best there have also been days when I have, because I was watching the race closely so that I might have some luck explaining it to my son, because the rest of the crowd had not entirely forgotten her, because moments of true appreciation are profound, because the gods sometimes bless us, I watched with pride as the last runner came down the homestretch.

After the race, I leaned over and told my son that what makes track special is that the runner who finishes last is doing the exact same thing as the runner who finishes first. It doesn't get any better than that.

The Secret

We don't tell beginners
but the first mile
is what every subsequent mile will be:
one foot in front of the other.

Like time itself
marked by the entropy
of your days.

First your shoe
then your knees or hips
or back
when you began
trusting that it would get easier—

the faith of the long-distance runner.

Rewarded by hours and miles
alone
with the same tired doubts
you harbored in your youth
saturating your flickering consciousness
until necessity subsumes
the fibers of—
it's okay, call it
Being

what you are
doing.

Like the secret no one
needed to tell
your muscles—
exhale foot strike foot strike foot strike inhale
foot strike foot strike exhale.
It does get easier
—and harder—
this running

for the joy of running
a million miles from here
if you're lucky
you'll be right where you are now.

I Said Go

Go. Go and keep going. Go until your time is up, which it soon will be. Like life? Yes, just like life. What brings you to this run? God, the universe, history? Let's call it luck. It doesn't matter. Here you are. Have you arrived? If you are practicing, you are practicing what? If running is devotional, you are devoting yourself to what? Commitment—same question. Do you come to running to meet yourself, to acquaint with facts, with biology, with body? To confront reality, to prepare for death? Would you say that when you chase after yourself, you elude yourself, too? Legs on a snake, ouroboros on the run. Only running, really running, may you arrive at the Hindu notion of lila—to play is to play. So, go, play. I said go. What are you waiting for? Go. I said go.

The Very First Thing

I rise to meet the sun
sounds like something a runner would say
if he wanted to impress someone
most likely himself.

I rise to meet the sun
he says proudly
summoning the life and renewal
—and truth? yes!—and truth
he's sure are inside him.

I rise to meet the sun
he writes again
starting to wonder if enough
is enough already
if his running shorts still fit.

Could he still do it
he wonders. Could he
find his shoes in the back closet?
Could he stop
writing about the sunrise
long enough to go and
in his words
"meet it"?

Worry not, reader,
our runner is brave, bold;
he can and he will
meet the sunrise
first thing tomorrow,
very first thing.

Get ready.

On Running or Not Running
the Portland Marathon

Feet don't hurt until they do.

I might have found this out years ago
reading Wittgenstein
but I'm a slow learner
better with bones than books.

No stress
fracture
the doctor can confirm in the x-rays
but that doesn't mean
there isn't one there he says
leading us
deep into the Rumsfeldian territory
of known & unknown unknowns.

But the territory I want to explore isn't abstract
it's Portland
where I'm registered to run the marathon
in two months
for the first time
in twelve years.

Seven hard miles

on fast cement
and no shoes
is the only metaphysics that matters
now. I don't doubt

my pain I can't
run or find my way home
to the unknown known
of Portland rain some fall
when feet meet ground & there is nothing more

not to know.

Not Running as a Spiritual Practice

The white lines of my bones are bright and solid on the x-rays. No stress fracture visible, although my physical therapist sister has warned me they don't always show up in the pictures. My doctor doesn't know what's causing the pain in my foot. Neither do I. I do know approximately when it started: a few weeks ago. And I know exactly how long it's been since I ran: since Saturday.

Saturday was a test. It followed ten days of deliberate rest. Prior to that I tried to run through the pain, telling myself it was okay, that it'd just work itself out the way it usually did. As it turned out, the pain did not work itself out. So, for the first time I can remember in twenty years of running, intentional rest. And then Saturday's test to see if ten days had been enough. I made it two miles pain-free into a four-mile run. Then I noticed my left foot landing tenderly. Then I felt a big warm sensation signaling trouble spreading across my foot. Nothing dramatic, just a clear declaration, *You want to pay attention to this.* I knew it was serious—or at least potentially so—at the end of the four miles only because of how tired my right quad was. It felt, due to the extra work it was doing, like it'd been through a half marathon or more. The foot pain itself wasn't severe, just persistent in its strange vague way.

This wasn't how I saw the summer going. Just before my foot started hurting, I'd signed up to run the Portland Marathon in the fall. It was to be my first time back to the race (now put on by a new organization and following a new and, to my mind, much improved course) in twelve years and my first marathon at all in six.

After a mostly dormant winter, my running year got off to a good start in the late spring. It was still snowing into June in Montana, but there were plenty of nice days to start getting in miles. It's always a process for my body to learn how to run again after the long winter. My legs feel awkward, like they're not entirely sure where to land or what to do when my feet feel the ground. But within a few days I start to rediscover the rhythm of the run. From there it's a matter of gradually building miles and minutes. Speed, I always trust, will come back in time. Or not. The faster I can run comfortably the more fun running is, but speed is not the point. The point is only to be out there enjoying the feeling of moving my body in space. I like myself better when I'm running, and I think my wife likes me better, too. It's easier to like someone who likes life than someone who's always butting heads with it. And one thing I've noticed about running is that doing it makes me a happier, better version of myself. I feel lucky to be alive, lucky to have a body, lucky to be able to move it. I like the sun and the trees and even, as often as not, the wind. I like the rain. I like being tired. I like feeling energetic. I like going fast. I like going slow. Etc. Etc.

I had some good runs this summer. My first time going ten miles I ran hard on the uphills and breezed over the downhills, delighted to be moving with such power and freedom. I ran a hot, gruelling trail through Yellowstone and felt good and worn out when I finished. I ran a half-marathon that didn't go well but went well enough that when it was over I signed up for Portland.

And then one day soon after the half I ran a fast fives miles on pavement in flimsy sandals. The next day I ran seven in the same sandals. The day after that I noticed my foot hurting slightly. I took a few days off. I ran moderately for a couple weeks. My foot felt fine. Then I ran 38K over uneven ground in the Rocky Mountains. Two shorts runs after that followed my inception of the ten-day break and the Saturday test that became my last run of the summer.

It's common among runners to know running less as a form of physical exercise than as a way of being. Yet we have a hard time talking about it most of the time. Even when we broach the subject of running's mysterious pull on us, we tend to do so in the language of self-improvement. Running relieves anxiety! Running improves sleep! Running lifts self-confidence! Running works like meditation! Running is more effective than Prozac!

Maybe so. But it wouldn't matter a bit if running did none of those things. We runners run because we like running. It's as simple as that. And from this perspective, the excited claims made on running's behalf are reminiscent of someone proclaiming sex as a good way to burn calories. At best, running's purported beneficial side effects are ways of talking about what *like* means. Take the peace of mind that often attends running. Maybe running produces peace of mind, and maybe when I say I like running what I mean, in part, is that I like having this peace of mind. Even so, why reduce running to a method of producing an effect? It would be as if someone said of drinking that it reliably brings the pleasure of drunkenness. Some people, of course, drink this way. I remember being sixteen as well as anyone. But there are more refined attitudes toward alcohol that offer rewards unknown to anyone who drinks for the sake of being drunk. That's how running is. Peace of mind might be a feature of running, but it's not the goal. The goal of the type of running I'm interested in is only ever to run.

But why is that the goal, the non-runner may still wish to ask. *What is the intrinsic reward?* Let's see. Running brings me into the present moment. The worries and regrets I normally orient by fade from my attention. They don't vanish entirely, but they take a more appropriate place in the landscape of my interior. When I'm running I don't have to maintain my usual vigilance around the contingencies of life. I don't have to monitor every aspect of the day-to-day under the faulty but habitual assumption that such monitoring establishes control. Running makes me more aware of my surroundings. I am attuned to light, to color, to sound, to smells, to atmospheric conditions, to my breathing, to my thoughts, to my mood. Whatever I encounter or whatever arises in my experience during a run *is my experience of the run*. It sounds tautological, except that so much of life for me is not the experience of it but the thoughts about it. Running bypasses some of this default way of relating to the world. I would describe running as a feeling of inhabiting my body more fully than is normal if it weren't for the dualism inherent in *inhabit*; rather, running allows me to notice more easily that *I am my body* and, what's more, to notice that being a body is often a wondrous and delightful thing, even if—sometimes *especially* if—it is accompanied by some physical discomfort. But not *only a body*. All parts of me (whatever these parts are called, whatever these parts *are*) align on a run in the direction of happiness. A goal, then, happiness? No. Happiness is less a target to shoot for than the direction the runner is pulled. Before running is a cause of happiness, it is an expression of it.

Not that any of this is reliable. Bringing me into the present moment and my particular environment, unifying the various parts of me, expressing joy—these are tendencies not promises. Very often running is frustrating, disappointing, difficult but not pleasurable. That's a valuable part of it too, as it gives poignancy to those more inspired moments.

I ran for many years before it ever occurred to me to think about running as a spiritual practice. But now *spiritual practice* strikes me as a varied and nuanced enough term to capture the essence of what it means for a runner to be a runner.

That sounds like an overstatement, I understand. Here's what I'm thinking: the rewards of running are made possible only by effort and commitment. It is a practice one maintains. And if one maintains it, running can engage the whole of one's being and give purpose to that being. It becomes, when maintained, central to one's identity. And that identity, very often, is shared with a community of other runners.

That said, *spiritual practice* might still be a bit of a reach. It's too obvious that running can be nothing more than one part of an exercise routine. It can be treated as a form of necessary suffering that one mitigates through distracting music or the external reward of social media posts. So maybe it's too much to say that running is a spiritual practice—it's too capacious an activity for one classification. But maybe, too, a spiritual practice is one thing running can be.

How else are we to understand the spate of books like Mackenzie L. Harvey's *Mindful Running*, Gary Dudney's *The Tao of Running*, Sakyong Mipham's *Running with the Mind of Meditation*, Warren A. Kay's *Running: The Sacred Art*, Roger D. Joslin's *Running the Spiritual Path*, and on and on?

One thing you notice if you read such books is how common it is for runners to celebrate aspects of running that are not reducible to the purely physical act of propelling oneself quickly by foot. It's not just these authors, either, who notice the transcendent nature of the practice. It's the dozens of runners they profile in their books; it's the implication that anyone they haven't profiled would have a similar story to tell; it's the conversations you might have with anyone who runs regularly; it's the experiences you've likely had yourself if you've put even a moderate amount of time into running.

As my doctor examined my foot he said that he had to figure out how to help me recover *for my wife's sake*. His joke hit the mark. Since I had stopped running I had started having regular, almost daily, petty little fights with her. There were a few reasons at least that I was more irritable than usual. First, the frustration of being injured, which ran counter my notions of what I wanted and, frankly, *expected* the world to be. Second, the added stress of not knowing exactly what my injury was or how long it would take me to heal. This state of uncertainty was even more difficult for me to accept than the injury itself. Third, the simple fact of my not running. I was used to running daily, and the shock of suddenly stopping had me discombobulated. Mentally and emotionally, as well as physically, I didn't know how to adjust to not running, and my penned-in feeling was expressing itself as the negative energy I effused indiscriminately. For twenty years, running had been a source of well-being for me. Without it, I was floundering.

But as the weeks dragged on while I waited for my follow-up appointment with a specialist, I eventually let go of my hope to run the Portland Marathon that year (the race organizers kindly let me defer my registration until the next). That took off the pressure of a timeline, which then allowed me to accept that I might not run again for months. With each level of acceptance it became easier to embrace the life I was living rather than be bitter about the life I wasn't. How far could that extend?

Running, you meet yourself anew in struggle. Your limits are where you discover who you are. The environment impinges itself upon you. If you fight against the rain, the cold, the heat, or (toughest for me) the wind, you'll feel weak in comparison. The victim of your attack on conditions will be yourself. But if you can greet the same conditions with good spirits you can collaborate with them on creating the experience of the present moment. The same wind that frustrates me when I oppose myself to it becomes a neutral party when I let go my expectations of what I want my run to be like. I will run slower with a headwind than without one. The air may sting my skin. I may be knocked off my stride. So be it. When I run I have the opportunity to make peace with my situation.

The same must be true when I'm not running. The pain in my foot, vague as it is, focuses my attention to where and how I place it on the ground. The injury can bring my attention to the reality of my body and its environs just as running can. Even now, I can become aware that my left foot is tender and my right quad feels stressed, though less so than a few weeks ago. I can become aware of my mood (which helps reduce the number of petty fights I have with my wife) and my thoughts (frustrations about not running, but also gratitude for the injury not being any worse) and my limitations (which are inseparable from my abilities). Here's what I'm getting at: if running can be a spiritual practice, can't not running be one, too?

My appointment with the specialist is tomorrow. Maybe she'll be able to help me recover, and maybe she won't be. Either way, when I'm ready to run again, however long that is from now, I will. Until then, I won't. It sounds so simple. But what I'm appreciating is that just about everything I need to know about how I want to be in the world is contained in that simple fact. When I can run, I will. Until then, I won't.

While I'm not running, there's plenty I can do. I can sit in this chair. I can focus my attention on my foot and see how it feels this morning. I can observe, as I might when running, the particular nature of the unique moment I am in—the way the wind is blowing through the window, the way the sky is tinged pink just after sunrise, the way the coffee tastes today, the way writing works on my attention, the way it comes as a relief to notice a degree of buoyancy in my mood. I can wait to recover. I can be patient. I can be content. It might take practice, but I am confident today, sitting in this chair watching the pink sky turn blue, that I can be myself in not running just as much as I can in running. It is a new practice. It is a more challenging practice. And like all practices, it takes effort and commitment. For the time being, I don't have the choice to run. And as long as I'm not running it will be up to me if I will make the effort to practice not running. If my twenty years of running have taught me anything, it's that when there is something I can do that makes me feel like myself, I owe it to myself to do it. And if practicing not running can do that right now, not running is what I'm committed to.

Life Is Luck
A Defense of Galen Rupp

It is not unreasonable to imagine that Galen Rupp will one day be made to forfeit his medals, his records, and what remains of his legacy in the aftermath of the revelations regarding his coach's laxity around ethical sport.

If and when that day comes, what should the reaction be? To think about that, let's imagine ourselves into that future in which Rupp's name has been striked from the record books like Ben Johnson, Lance Armstrong, Marion Jones, and so many others before him. The first honest thing we will have to say is that he deserved what he got. He had it coming. There's no place in sport for cheaters. Every child knows that.

Except, if children do learn not to cheat, how?

Nothing I am on my way to arguing is meant to exculpate Rupp from the consequences of his actions. But the question I want to raise is whether we should *blame* him for those actions.

Back in 1990s Portland, I was a boy who liked sports. Basketball was my favorite then, but I played them all. There were hundreds of boys like me, thousands. One of them was a few years younger than me and lived a few miles from my house. He and I would play soccer on the same rainy fields. As teenagers, we would run the same races. We had a lot in common—this other boy, me, all of us.

But while many of us share similar sporting backgrounds, few among us would truly excel in sports. The other boy in this parable—Rupp, of course—was one who would. It might have been in soccer, a sport at which he was already considered one of the best in

Oregon. "But then," as he would later put it in an interview, "lucky for me, I crossed paths with Alberto."

Luck is right. Life is luck. Rupp, already genetically gifted, happened to enroll at the one high school where Alberto Salazar was coaching. Salazar, on the lookout for talented young runners he could cultivate to world success, saw in this high school freshman what must have looked like destiny.

But imagine how easily Rupp's life could have gone differently. Say he'd gone to his district public school instead of Central Catholic. Maybe he would have been the best runner on his soccer team but never entered a race. Say Central Catholic just happened to be coached by anyone but Salazar. Say Salazar hadn't been notified that there was a kid on the soccer team who could run. If things were different, the saying goes, they wouldn't be the same.

We might be tempted here to say that these counterfactuals get us nowhere. Who cares what didn't happen? All that matters is what did. I'm tempted in this direction. In a way, I think it's right. But what I notice is that whatever did happen *happened to Rupp*. He wasn't the cause of his talent, Salazar's presence, or Salazar's interest in him. He was a kid who happened to be fast.

What is agency? Galen Rupp was a child when Alberto Salazar entered his life. He was a child when Salazar began grooming him for success. He was a child when Salazar became a father figure to him. He was a child when he began to see himself through Salazar's eyes. We would not hold the fourteen-year-old Rupp responsible for Salazar's influence. What about the eighteen-year-old who was allowed to train with his own private coach instead of under the team's coach? What about the twenty-six-year-old Olympian who had been Salazar's preferred athlete for over a decade? In the context of his relationship with Salazar, when, exactly, is agency meant to have coalesced for Rupp?

Put yourself in Rupp's spikes: Of all the boys playing soccer in Portland, Alberto Salazar—the Alberto Salazar— singles you out for distinction, tells you there is promise in your legs, tells you he can make you an Olympian. Can you imagine how natural it would have been, as a child, to fall under the spell of someone so charismatic, so confident, so accomplished? And then everything he promises you comes true: NCAA champion, Olympic medalist, the face of American distance running. Every time he says "Trust me," you trust him. And look where it gets you. Look where you are. You wouldn't apply the cream he told you to apply? You wouldn't take the prednisone he told you to take?

It's easy to be sanctimonious from the safety of mediocrity. It is only in imagination that we can walk, never mind *run*, a mile in Rupp's shoes. But when we do imagine ourselves in his place, can we really be so sure we would conduct ourselves differently?

Kara and Adam Goucher, former teammates of Rupp's and two of the key whistleblowers against Nike Oregon Project's rampant flouting of the rules under Salazar's direction, are among the moral heroes of this story. Galen Rupp is not. But the standard for excellence should be as high in morality as it is in athletics. Not everyone achieves it. But whereas in the athletic sphere we readily neglect our also-rans, in the moral sphere we can choose to embrace our mediocrities. Rupp is no hero, but he's no villain, either. If most of us have something in common with him, it is this: our moral mediocrity. The reaction Rupp's example should elicit from us is not condemnation but compassion.

Life is luck. But the thing about luck is it's often ambiguous. What first looks like the right genes falling into the right environment can, upon consideration, appear something much more tragic: bad luck dressed as success, fame, riches and the sinister grin of the Nike swoosh.

Behold the Runner
A View from the Pandemic

Most evenings lately, after we get our son down for the night, my wife and I retire to the bed and bring up a running documentary on her laptop. These evenings, as the new reality dictates, follow long days involving the two of us trading off between childcare (he's three) and trying to get some work done from home, and the best thing we've found to do with them is plop down and watch other people run around in the woods.

The quality of the documentaries is somewhat uneven, as they tend to be produced by runners experimenting with film as often as by filmmakers interested in running. But this hardly matters. Maybe it's even part of the appeal. We aren't cinephiles when we plop down, just two people who are tired and a little stressed and ready to be reminded what it's like to have both energy and the freedom to expend it. These films do us good.

My working thesis is that it is the movement that matters. To watch human beings propel themselves through natural landscapes seems to allow a kind of bodily empathy to be aroused. We feel as if we are running with them. Supine in our bed, in our minds we are striding and climbing and turning and adjusting and going and going and going. It's like a dream, even, one that produces a deep and primordial joy in us. Like a dream, but visceral and real to the core. We run vicariously as the films' protagonists chase their arbitrary goals (set the record, complete the trail, summit the peak), knowing all along that the true purpose of running is only ever to be a body in motion through space. It's what we do. It's who we are.

When I open up the news app on my phone, it insists on showing me headlines about some person who ran some incredible distance in their backyard. It saddens me even to contemplate that this is what it's come to. I have ignored each such story I've been presented with, yet day after day more of them appear. It's enough to make me want to buy a treadmill.

I have been a lucky runner during the pandemic. I have run almost every day of lockdown without a mask. My town isn't densely populated, our incidence rate is low, and when I do encounter someone else out and about there's plenty of time to execute a distancing maneuver.

At home, it's the three of us. I can't remember the last time we met someone else in person. We hardly have anywhere to go. Days—no, weeks—have passed without me leaving the house for anything but my daily run. I can't say I've come to count on running. That's been true for too many years to count now as a revelation. But I might appreciate running more than ever. I don't want to say running is keeping me sane (that's better left for my wife to say), but it is keeping me something like steady. I put on my shoes and feel a sense of intrigue about the world. I start out from our house and feel the stress of the pandemic begin to lift. As my legs loosen, so do my tangled thoughts. Joy visits me. Some days, anyway, joy visits me. I run like the sun shines. My feet barely touch the ground. And when I'm done I am happy or tired or full of love for my wife and son and full of gratitude that we are all healthy. Or all of these at once.

And then my son wants to run across the backyard to the fence and back and suddenly that isn't a sad thing to do but a beautiful thing, full of joy and meaning. We run and laugh and play so much these three things have become inseparable to me, synonyms in essence.

And at night, because I am happy and my body is tired in just the right way and our boy is asleep on the mat he has pulled alongside our bed, I signal to my wife that there's a running documentary we haven't seen yet. We plug in headphones and start the film and behold once again a human body fully alive in its environment doing what it was made to do. We watch those runners moving themselves over the land and we think none of this will be forever, none of it.

Family Reunion

Brother and sister together again,
both of us stiff now with injury and age,
but running still, or something like it.

We would be unrecognizable
to our younger, swifter selves,
who wouldn't look back if they could.

Fine for them, and fine for us
back here where everything is
as it is supposed to be, where we are
keeping the steady pace of decline.

Short Poems

it can't be a coincidence
there are twenty-six bones
in the human foot

// /

how lucky
to be a runner
or anything at all

//

when the snow melts
and underneath it
footprints

//

a run
like a blossom
on the branch of an old tree

//

just running
through the hurt of life
like a falling leaf

//

I used to run races with my legs
now I rely on experience
to get me to the finish line

says a voice in my head
to an audience of none
as I disappear over the horizon

//

there's nothing wrong
with Montana
than an early
summer trail
run can't cure

//

fast he ran
then faster

till time
stopped

for him
alone

eternally
in eternity

where he was
for a time

the fastest
one

//

running in the spring
the kid has rain water
in his veins

// /

meet me in the body
meet me in the bones

we are a lot alike
you and I, animals

creaturely in meat
and marrow, we

know the miles as well
as they know us

// /

oh legs!
oh thousands
upon thousands
of miles!

// /

cloud of breath
in the air—cold
body on the move

/ /

out for a run
in the early morning streets
just me and the world

/ /

"Wherever you go,
there you are." —John Kabat-Zinn
and me when I run

/ /

peaceful run with love
for all god's creatures—even you
red-winged blackbird

//

a running senryū
in which the feet fall to earth
according to feel

//

twenty miles of trail
never taking me an inch
from myself

//

I don't want to run
a run I don't want to run
or write about it

//

hungry up early
my legs have teeth
and I eat miles

//

wind at my back
a better version of myself
running down the road

//

a beautiful thing
to watch your kid run and be
his own sacred yes

//

are you all sweaty
asks the younger boy, laughing
at run-crazy dad

//

lonely runner
on lonely trail
horizon everywhere

//

yellow and purple
flowers in the prairie grass
—runner coming through!

//

one sunny afternoon
running the same old trails
a new turnoff appears

//

running in the ocean
with my boy
like when I was a boy

// /

running
the ridgeline
with mountain goat confidence

// /

top of the mountain
if I leap—
only clouds

// /

running in the rain
alone in my element

On Possibly Becoming
a Middle-Aged Doper

I turned forty and showed up for my physical ready to be surprised. But the prostate exam was nothing like these words out of my doctor's mouth: "You should be taking your Albuterol before every run, especially this time of year."

It wasn't totally crazy. I have some breathing trouble. I have a prescription for a drug that relieves my breathing trouble. The logic nearly does itself.

But do I need the treatment? Like, really need it? And if I don't need it, how can I justify taking it? And so I fall once again into the bottomless pit of self-analysis.

Do I need Albuterol?

Clearly not. I've been running for almost twenty years since I was first prescribed Albuterol after being rushed to the hospital with a severe asthma attack. Except for in the aftermath of that event, when I was recovering, I haven't taken the drug. I'm still running. I'm still alive. Therefore, I don't need the drug.

But should I be taking it anyway?

Not dying is fine and well, but can I rightly stake a claim to something better for myself? What am I trying to prove to whom by not taking a drug that would make my life better? I take Tylenol and caffeine to make my life better. Why not Albuterol?

Who am I?

I am a person who sometimes gets headaches. So: Tylenol. I am a person who enjoys enhancing my mental clarity and alertness. So:

caffeine. I could go on in the direction of drugging to alter consciousness, but the point wouldn't change: I do it because I like it.

Do I also like breathing easily?

I do. So, again, what's the problem? While I don't mind thinking of myself as a person who sometimes gets headaches, I do mind thinking of myself as asthmatic. I was in my twenties when I had the incident that resulted in my diagnosis of allergy-induced asthma. Because of that late age, I never internalized the diagnosis. I have always considered the whole episode to be more a fluke than something that refers to me in a meaningful way. In the same way I don't think of myself as someone with vision trouble, even though I've been wearing glasses for fifteen years, I don't think of myself as having asthma. Inside, I'm still young, breathing well, seeing 20/20.

The evidence suggests otherwise.

I know, I know. I should take the drug. I want to.

What's the problem?

The problem is I want to take it so that I will run faster.

It could be that I'd run faster because my airways wouldn't be constricted anymore.

Maybe. Or maybe whatever state my airways would otherwise be in, Albuterol will open them. My performance will be improved relative to my previous performance, but it could also be that my performance would be improved relative to whatever "normal functioning airways" is supposed to refer to. My breathing is part of my running in the same way that anyone's genetics are part of theirs. There is no clear distinction in my mind between taking a drug to treat a medical condition and taking a drug to enhance performance. Nor do I think any such distinction could ever be made any way but arbitrarily.

Maybe I shouldn't be such a philosopher. My doctor wants me to take a drug so I won't be wheezing after every run. My wife worries when she hears the sounds my chest makes. Maybe it's time to shut up and take the medicine.

Except I don't think I'm being a philosopher here. I think I'm trying to say that even though I literally have a doctor's note, it feels like cheating.

It's not that I don't think my drug use would be medically warranted. It's that, nevertheless, I would suspect myself of gaining an advantage that I could have declined to gain. And that feels to me like something a virtuous person would not do.

Did I really just say "virtuous person"?

I'm afraid I did. But I wouldn't defend this sense of virtue on philosophical grounds. Quite the opposite. If I were being a philosopher here, I'd first try to trouble the concept of natural as ambiguous to the point of meaninglessness. I'd point in the directions of individual difference, of uncertainty, of multiple causes and confounding variables. I'd point insistently in the direction of luck. I'd point to all those things. And in the end, I'd still feel like I was cheating.

What can I attribute that to?

I think I should be a better philosopher, one with the courage of my convictions. But when I look deep within what I might call my soul I see these remnants of a long-dead religion: the linked convictions that the self is a stable thing and that to opt too easily out of suffering is to do oneself a moral disservice.

Maybe I am sick, after all.

Running, Metaphor, and the Self
On Rickey Gates's *Cross Country*

At one level, running is a means of getting from here to there. But this simple, physical observation gets complicated as soon as we notice that the person who arrives over there isn't the same person who departed from here. It may be difficult to appreciate this transformation when the run is a short sprint to catch the bus or a leisurely jog around the neighborhood, so consider how some runners approach a first marathon. It becomes for them an occasion on which to throw themselves into uncertainty. The territory they are exploring is new, their success unassured. These runners—sure that, succeed or fail, the experience will change them—make explicit two truths that are otherwise implicit: that the self is not a stable thing and that when we talk about running we talk about metaphor.

And when we talk not about running to the corner or a few miles or even about 26.2 miles but about running across the United States, the psychological implications become obvious: whoever Rickey Gates is in South Carolina, he will be someone else when he reaches California. Five months and 3,700 miles ensure it.

I had questions for *Cross Country*. Who is Gates? A professional trail runner, it turns out. One possibly in the twilight of his career who, having broken up with his girlfriend, feels directionless in life. Why does he want to run across the country? To find some metaphorical direction and to gain a better understanding of his country. Who does he want to become? He doesn't know. How could he? A person cannot imagine himself as another self for the simple reason that when he becomes another self he will no longer be the prior self. To become is to cease to be. Change is assured but no one who changes.

To live is to be perpetually falling off the cliff of existence—or to be always running across the country of discovery.

What happens along the way? According to Gates:

> Oftentimes, we don't have the capacity to recognize our own personal growth or decomposition—it's a realization that's reserved for reunions, weddings, and funerals. Occasionally, though, it's drastic. The flu, followed by dehydration, long miles, and rising temperatures, chiseled away at the last of my fat and into my muscle. In a culvert, beneath the Loneliest Road in America, the abyss was staring back at me.

That abyss, Nietzsche's abyss, waits there for any of us who dare face it. Those who do, Gates shows us, will by revealed to themselves. Where they thought they always had been, they will find instead the universe, the cold, dark, enchanted universe, its light ricocheting back and forth as between two mirrors facing and summoning again an infinite something out of nothing.

It can look like that: "The stars began to appear, and then the Milky Way, and then one, two, three shooting stars. In the darkness, it was nearly impossible to see the far end of that maddening stretch of road, so instead I focused on the few faint feet that I could see just ahead of me."

On the long journey toward becoming yourself, you begin where you are and you never go anywhere else.

Running with Your True Self Before You Were Born

A Koan, an Essay, A Reality

The Zen of Running was published in 1974 through a collaboration between Random House and The Bookworks, a New Age press out of Berkeley that published three other books (on massage, organic gardening, and alternatives to public education) in the few years of its operation. The author of *The Zen of Running*, Fred Rohé, who died in 2023, was a natural foods guru, whose Palo Alto store is unofficially credited as being the inspiration for Whole Foods. He wrote several books on food and diet but after his debut never returned to the subject of running.

As this context would suggest, to pick up *The Zen of Running* is to find oneself barefoot in 1970s California. I, for one, cannot study the black and white images of the author's long, lean, and nearly naked body moving easily through natural settings and not see some possible elemental version of myself in his form. If not for his commitment to the fashions of the time, Rohé could be running straight out of pre–jean shorts, pre-headband prehistory. And I could be running there with him, if only I were a bit longer, a bit leaner, and could move a bit more easily.

But that's not the invitation, is it—to assume Rohé's elegant lines. The real invitation is internal—to feel what Rohé feels. That's the promise, too: that inside each of us is an essence that can be both discovered and expressed by moving our bodies steadily through space in a way our ancestors would have recognized.

What I have in mind when I invoke our deep past isn't persistence hunting per se or delivering messages over long distances but the rightness of function fitted to form. Put yourself in your running body and it is possible to know with the confidence of a parent's love that you were made for this. And then what but gospel truth can you call Rohé's unadorned verse?

> *don't overdo it.*
> *underdo it.*
> *you aren't running because*
> *you're in a hurry to get somewhere*

To encounter lines like these—in calligraphy, no less—is to be immersed in an aesthetic of inspiration and optimism. It is to be returned, whether one was ever there, to a time when it was possible to speak of human potential without cynicism and to believe that private revelations could be made to endure.

Of course, there's the temptation for those of us who know this hippie history only through the nostalgic distortions of popular culture to dismiss such optimism as naïve and declare it all but unthinkable for ours and subsequent generations. As well, there's the temptation to lament our lateness upon the scene. Regardless of its eventual failure, how good it would have felt to be there, to know such innocence, to look straight ahead with the gleam of an Eastern guru in our eye. But either temptation denies the possibility of Rohé-like freedom being available right here, right now. And I must tell you: I think it is. For, as unlikely as it may be, I have known such freedom myself. And I have known it at those moments in my life that I take to be my sanest. By which I mean that I have known it on psilocybin, I have known it on ecstasy, I have known it in love, and I have known it on those occasions when I have been able to reside deep in my running body and, simultaneously, in my right mind. It is there, where the oneness of all things is manifest, that I have even experienced a kind of peace that I recognize as absolute and divinely patient.

There, I've told you. Now, let me add that part of me would happily ride these mystical rhythms all the way through to the end of this essay and throw in my lot with Rohé when he writes,

> *I mean that meditation is a state of being,*
> *not a physical position.*
> *I can run in a state that is just as meditative,*
> *perhaps more so,*
> *than when sitting Buddha-like.*

I could conclude grandly with the proclamation that *The Zen of Running* offers nothing less than a way of life as wise as that of any philosophy or religious tradition; that it offers a means by which we might become fully human.

But another part of me remains skeptical. By stripping running down to its barefoot and near-naked essence, and by assuming (not without good evidence) that running in this way brings us close to the essence of what the human body does, Rohé gives the impression of having led us close to our very human essence. Except, there is running, and then there is running.

Sticking safely to the long hair of the early seventies, Steve Prefontaine embodied the essence of running his own way. Frontrunning at the far-right tail of human excellence, Pre's example symbolizes not just the limits of what is possible but the possibility of surpassing such limits. Take as representative of Prefontaine fandom three lines from Bill Pearlman's poem "3:55":

> *Pushing it all aside, he is in heaven*
> *Eugene opens all its gentle heart*
> *To see this frontrunner miling against time alone.*

This poem appears in Pearlman's chapbook *An Elegy for Prefontaine and Other Track Poems*, another small-press gem of the decade, this one published in 1977 by Living Batch Press of Albuquerque in an edition of 300 copies. Pearlman is interested in the greatness and the legend of Prefontaine. He acknowledges that it was the greatness that birthed the legend and the legend that survives the man and the greatness that belong to the past.

Death is always close
to such a whirrld—
he who would hold attention
whose body commanded fidelity
who took away the laurels
was only human
though we would have it otherwise—

. . .

We wanted him out front
speeding into a new dimension
our selves hanging on the shirttails

No honest fan of Pre's would deny this claim, but so rarely do we ask why the need for him to be what we cannot be. Why Pearlman's need? Why so many's? Why mine?

This is supposed to be an essay attesting to the rewards of being true to one's individual nature, but Pre threatens that premise. We could say that in his rarefied excellence he was simply being who he happened to be, and this is no doubt true as far as it goes. But we don't look to Pre for this reason alone. Rather, we look to him because he flew so flagrantly in the face of resistance, as if he were personally affronted by the constraints of reality. Aren't we a long way from Zen in our admiration for the abandon of Pre's running? Wasn't his kind of running actually a form of violence? And wasn't this violence what constituted his magnetic beauty? Look at him on the track, carrying out a war of self against world. Witness him subjecting himself unceasingly to a test of his indefatigable will. As inspired as we onlookers may be, few among us really attempt what he was attempting. No, inspiration takes another form here. The fact of Pre's existence enchants our world. We needn't aspire to his greatness to be grateful that by some miracle he once ran among us.

It is that fine religious line he tracked between the human and the beyond that inspires our devotion. As foreign as his accomplishments would be to most humans who have ever lived, we know, finally, as does Pearlman, that even the mythological Prefontaine must give way to the existential reality of existence:

> *It is ourselves dying*
> *and we stand at the edge of the unknown*
> *neither victorious nor defeated, alone*

Still, how to reconcile the tension between acceptance and ambition, between being who you are and being as great as you can be? This is the tug-of-war I have been playing against myself for decades in my thinking about running. On the one hand, my spiritual inclination is with Rohé. On the other hand, I sometimes, when thinking of Pre, feel like I've let myself down in not getting the most out of my talents. That personal record that my memory returns to more often than you'd think and more often than I'd care to admit, it could have been faster. How much faster? If I have made peace with my running efforts in my heart, my mind is still somewhat eager to hector me about unfulfilled promise.

Strangely, I may have found a response to satisfy even my most self-punishing instincts in an analogy drawn from Susan Wolf's 1982 journal article "Moral Saints" (an analogy, by the way, that Wolf discourages me from drawing). Substituting my athletic terms for her moral ones yields a surprising thesis: "I believe that [athletic] perfection, in the sense of [obsessive athletic devotion], does not constitute a model of personal well-being toward which it would be particularly rational or good or desirable for a human being to strive."

The problem I would like to channel from Wolf is that it's the single-mindedness of pursuing excellence that crowds out other goods. Would I want to have run a faster personal best if it had come at the cost of unburdened time with my wife or the years I idled away on quixotic artistic pursuits? How much would I want to care about preparing for my next marathon in a life with children and students and a dozen other interests?

But so maximizing my running potential isn't an especially high priority for me. Is Wolf making a normative claim in her critique of moral sainthood? Am I making one here in distancing myself from Prefontaine? Here is Wolf, making clear to me what I've intuited all along: "I have not meant to condemn the [athletic] saint or the person who aspires to become one. Rather, I have meant to insist that the ideal of [athletic] sainthood should not be held as a standard against which any other ideal must be judged or justified, and that the posture we take in response to the recognition that our lives are not as [athletically] good as they might be need not be defensive."

That's right. Despite the forces of Nike ad campaigns, despite our national obsession with dominance, I don't have to measure myself against the likes of Prefontaine. But that doesn't mean that Prefontaine was wrong to measure himself against his own impossible standards. What Wolf helps me see (is it always the most obvious things that are hardest to see?) is that I don't need a philosophical justification to be myself. The human being is a multitude. If we are to speak of essence, we must make this acknowledgment. And because we are a multitude, there are myriad humans I cannot be: Pre, for one; everyone else, as well. The only one I can be is the one I cannot not be. And my only essence lies in my own particularity. Once again, regardless of where I start, I end up in the same place: recognizing the impossibility of needing to become who I already am, the necessity of turning being and becoming into two ways of saying the same thing. It's all so paradoxical. At least it sounds paradoxical to me writing right now. But I know that sometimes when I'm running and the gap between what I am and what I think collapses there is no paradox at all.

So how about a final word on normativity? I'll say this: the world I want to live in is the world in which each of us thrives uniquely and without apology. It is the world in which Rohé and Pearlman sit side by side on my bookshelf, the world in which I model myself neither on Rohé nor Prefontaine but on some wild vision of myself that I will only ever encounter in its expression, never beforehand and never fully in retrospect. The race has not yet been run. The race will never be run. The race is always being run. There are no winners, no losers, only runners, all of us belonging right where are at the precise pace we're moving.

Three Elegies for Kelvin Kiptum

1. The News

We already knew the news was bad news when we saw the words "World-Record Marathoner" appear on our screens late in the American evening, Rotterdam two months in the distance. And then the word "Car" and the word "Accident" and the thoughts of Prefontaine, unconscious for now, readying themselves for their eventual burst into awareness. It's a rare feat to reach terminal velocity: disappearing while still just arriving. We knew him only a year, saw him run only three times—and that's if we were watching, which mostly we weren't, since we hadn't yet realized we needed to, our equations still failing to explain Kipchoge, now suddenly half a minute more human. If you can outrun possibility, why not the laws of physics? Or is Kiptum the solution to that ancient riddle: the irresistible force no match for the immovable object? We know about mortality and the vanity of our affairs and how our lives are like a wind passing from nowhere to nowhere, know them as well as we are strong to see. Yet the news when it comes is bad news. It's so easy at that moment to overlook the good news that creation, too, is always ongoing. But we can look back and see, we can look back and see, we can look back and see, and when we're feeling brave extrapolate.

2. Countdown

Wouldn't it be so easy to write of beauty and courage
and strength and grace and endurance and all the characteristics
composing *essence*, and wouldn't it be so easy to write of the void
that engulfs being—engulfs and subsumes—yet so much harder

to keep in mind both at once while day after death after day
life is chewed in the teeth of destruction and we are left here

after sunset to fiddle around with words, I mean feelings.

3. April 21, 2024

Let's remember him
    running
      like water
        like morning light
    down every street—
      thought
        giving chase
          only after
      when the best of us
        the unexpected and improbably
            great had already
                lept.

Running Poem

The rhythm
is in
your feet
the way
they land
one
after a
nother un
til the run
is o
ver.

The Way to Run

Pushing the stroller
on the last sunny afternoon
of autumn
with you reaching
up to high five
me through
the small plastic window
in the covering
as we laugh
and then surge
for home
like we know
exactly
where we belong.

Today

I went for a run
to clear my head
not my mind.
This wasn't about
runaway thoughts
or a mood
that needed lifting.

I went for a run
to have the top of my head
taken off
like poetry did
for Dickinson.

I went for a run
to let my head be replaced
with the very world,
to notice
that there was nothing
for me to notice,

that Wittgenstein was right
the world is everything
that is the case
and that running is
sometimes the case.

Come What May

Each stride
like each breath
like the rain falling
or the sun rising
confirms
that what
comes   goes

and that I
always on my way
to where I am
going
have already
arrived.

Going Down Together

I love the looks
on people's faces
when they see us coming
down the mountain
like there's a bear behind us,
you bouncing on my shoulders
like you're in the toddler rodeo
shouting "faster like baxter"
as I try not to send us
barreling into the brush.

I refuse to stop
until you say so,
it being my sworn oath
to let you jump on beds
and climb up slides
and run down mountains
with your shoes untied
until you can't breathe
to teach you that form
and function are fungible,
that too often fear is just
self-imposed violence,
that an adult can remember
how much a child can feel.

I can't promise we won't fall,
but if we go down
we're going down
together.

Thinking with Your Legs

Do my legs deceive me? They do not.

My legs tell no lies, have never led me astray.

Legs do not represent the world, they encounter it.

They navigate the territory, not the map.

While the mind tends toward abstraction, feet stay close to the ground.

There is no runner who aspires to objectivity.

The runner knows that three miles isn't three miles.

Three miles is what you're capable of on a given run, whoever you are that day.

There's three miles and then there's three miles.

The runner knows from experience, knows it in the legs.

A good runner is a phenomenologist, where good means nothing more than fluency in the language of legs.

If a runner could speak, only a runner could hear.

"There is more reason in your body than in your best wisdom."
                    —Nietzsche's Zarathustra, def poet

Speaking of Nietzsche, imagine if the person who wrote "All truly great thoughts are conceived while walking" had had the good fortune to take up jogging.

Is the runner a materialist?—no—the runner is a runner.

Not embodiment, just bodiment.

It's not enough to listen to the body; you must be the body.

For the runner, the body is how the distributed mind thinks.

The runner knows that if thinking is something the body does, the body is just one of its thoughts.

And round and round the trail leads.

The runner is going nowhere, but the runner is going.

The legs will see to this.

Is the runner an idealist?—no—the runner is a runner.

The legs access deep memory. Every prior run is stored in the memory of the body.

It goes back as far as you would care to go, and farther.

Thinking like running is contingent upon the particular legs and their history running back to creation.

Why is there something rather than nothing? Because: the runner.

It takes two legs to run: neither rationalism nor empiricism can propel us forward. they must be coordinated.

Mind your legs as you leg your mind.

When we think with our legs there is no gap between us and the world, between mind and body, between knowing and doing.

Like the fish who forgot how to swim or the second baseman who can no longer make the throw to first, a runner can lose trust in their legs.

With luck, they will eventually remember (note the metaphor in remember) that ideas do not run, bodies run—legs.

To run freely is to think clearly.

Are My Best Miles Behind Me?

I had last run a timed mile eleven years before. In fact, I had run two timed miles that year, the first in the high 5:40s, the second in the low 5:40s. Prior to that, I don't know if I'd ever run a timed mile. Maybe once during high school soccer. I remember that our coach put us out on the track one day for a time trial and that I placed third on the team (and not very close to Bill Schaumberg or Justin Dreyer, either), but I'm not sure of the distance. It could have been a mile; it could have been two.

In any case, after eleven years, running in the heart of middle age, it occurred to me that perhaps I had become too precious about running, too satisfied with thinking about it in the quasi-mystical terms of nature aligned with nature. From a certain angle, my ongoing celebrations of running's subjective dividends could be seen as an excuse to ignore the core truth that to practice a skill is to work to improve oneself with respect to that skill, which in running usually means going faster.

What if, after all the years of proclaiming enlightened indifference toward results, really, I was scared—scared to find out how good I could be and how good I couldn't be? My competitive side found voice, taunting me that I was as deluded as someone who rejects a prize he was never offered, declines an invitation he never received. Either I would have to run fast (as fast as I could) or I could not be trusted when I claimed that running fast (as fast as one can) is beside the point. My credibility was at stake, my credibility with myself.

It didn't take all that much self-goading before I decided to give it a shot and see if I could still run a mile in under six minutes. Short story short: I could. It took me eight attempts over the course of two-plus months running weekly or biweekly laps by myself around a nearby high school track. In my first attempt, I ran 6:30. In subsequent attempts I shaved off a few or sometimes several seconds a go until the day I hit 5:58.

Recalling these events more than half a year removed from them, I notice a temptation to succumb to narrative expectations here and report that it felt good to reach my goal. It didn't. It felt like nothing, not even relief. That's not quite right, though. It was worse than that. The absence of a good feeling was itself a bad feeling. Upon finishing in 5:58, I understood the hollowness of this number. What difference did it make if I could or could not still run under 6:00?

By contrast, at my seventh attempt, on a day when I fully expected to come in under six but managed to run only 6:11, I felt disappointed, frustrated, crushed. What, I wondered following that run, was the point of this exercise? Why bother with this effort if it wouldn't pay off? And so on. Wouldn't it be better not to try to run fast than to try and fail? Wouldn't it be a more pleasant way to live, to not continue to subject myself to failure?

But a week after that disappointment, I showed up at the track again, made what felt like a similar effort, kept my splits somewhat more even, and crossed the line in 5:58, two seconds below the magic number, only to be immediately overcome with etterath, that particular feeling of emptiness that attends a goal achieved.

Runners know as well as anyone that it is easier to chase than to be chased. The thing that has been a source of meaning in your life vanishes as soon as you catch it, leaving you lost in the space between despair and new ambition. It wasn't the time itself but the pursuit of the time that had mattered. As Aristotle writes, "Man is a goal-seeking animal. His life only has meaning if he is reaching out and striving for his goals."

In other words, it would be possible for me to make my meaningless project meaningful again by taking it further. My 5:58 hadn't made me happy, but I could tell myself that another time would, knowing that if I ever reached the new goal I could just change it again to a still faster time. As long as I dangled the carrot of accomplishment (faster than before!) in front of my own eyes, I would always have something to chase.

Back in the race, my imagination took flight. Could I run sub-5:50? Maybe I could get a personal record? What was I still capable of? What wasn't I? Considering how uneven and unfocused my training had been, there was no reason that if I were to adhere to an established training program I shouldn't expect significant gains. And, to make things easier, I could find someone to race against instead of running solo. Given the paucity of my racing background, it was entirely reasonable that, despite my age, if I committed myself, my best mile could still be ahead of me.

So I talked myself temporarily out of etterath by promising myself a better time, with fulfillment to follow. Two weeks later, I made one more attempt at the mile and got my time down to 5:53. While this felt better than 5:58 had, it felt better only insofar as it portended something even better. No sooner had I registered my time than I was already borrowing from another imagined future to pay myself in the present. Though I was running on a track against the clock, my real race was to keep up with the hedonic treadmill that would never turn off.

In the long run, speed is a losing prospect. *He not still getting faster is already getting slower*, I sing to myself. It hadn't occurred to me when I accidentally set my mile PR at age thirty-two what it portended. As long as it held up as my PR, it meant I would never run as fast again. That's what a PR is: the height from which you will always, even if unevenly, be descending. And often we descend a fair distance before we look back and realize we've been at the top of our personal mountains.

So many elite runners, I've noticed, quit running when their competitive days are behind them. What's the point of running, their examples seem to suggest, if a person can no longer run fast? When I see these runners, I always wonder, did they enjoy running, or did they enjoy being good at something? I tell my children (as I tell myself) to pursue their interests, not their successes. Success is fleeting, whether it's objective of personal. But through dedication love can be maintained.

Whenever I think of practical Aristotle studying the character of human motivation, I think also of the romantic Aristotle claiming that the best kind of human life is one devoted to contemplation. A life so lived is not the means to some eventual end but the perfect expression of the innate characteristics of our species. Isn't it—can't it be—the same with running?

I'd like to tell myself that if I ever think my best miles are behind me, it is only because I have once again conflated *fastest* with *best*. If, instead, I can use *best* to refer to those that are ends in themselves because they express something profound in my nature, then my best mile will always be the one underfoot.

Of Miles

If you picture me,
picture me with miles
beneath my feet.

If you think of me,
think of me with so far yet to go,
how if I were here

I'd also be gone,
already on my way
toward the receding horizon

within. Imagine me
as you remember me:
indefatigable me,

still on my feet
—my moving feet—
after all these years.

Wherever you are, know
that I am here on the city streets
here on the trail through the woods.

I wish you could feel
these legs as I feel them,
speaking fluently with the miles they contain,

and feel the ground beneath these feet,
the way it moves as the world moves
in and out.

If these legs are old,
they are old enough
to have forgotten how to stop.

It has taken me thousands of miles,
thousands of miles
to get where I am:

the space between here
and there vast—
there is no going back.

If you think of me,
know that I am thinking of you
and what I'm saying is keep going,

eventually you will arrive.
Yes. And
how I wish you could join me

for these miles,
these miles that have led me
all the way into the distance.

WAVES

after Erwin Schrödinger

You come to the beach,
your familiar mass leaned
on the Sphinx's cane
as the sand gives ground.

There
in the distance
goes the tireless child
running
through the sea-salt air
like he's chasing the future
with intent
to surpass.

What if existence itself
is the true, the good, the beautiful?

If youth be fleeting,
child,
be fleet.

Momentum
is the only law
of metaphysics:
a body in motion

remains
in motion.

The back and forth
of sand and water,
sand and water, sand
and water,
all the wisdom
we can hope.

Count the waves
until numbers dissolve
into nonsense
and keep counting.

You ran on this beach
too when you were
young. So
just as effect
follows cause,
the wild
spray
of heels kicking
up surf
comprises a fractal
of actuality.

That boy,
is he
in fact
someone else?
Is he not by some
primordial
logic you?

Go gently,
then,
old man.

Tomorrow
is balanced
on the precipice
of a vast
emptiness.

Fragments from Fatherhood

Have you not watched the Olympics at the side of a two-year-old who can't stop, won't stop saying "Water jump!" until the race is over and he takes off for the backyard, where he is now naked, taking laps around the lawn, hurdling each time he passes into the kiddie pool chest first.

Have you not time and again taken exquisite joy in the boundless energy of children, the way their bodies serve as nature's expression of vitality.

Haven't you now and then watched a seven-year-old run three quarters of a mile on the track in his flip-flops and then kick those flip-flops off for the last lap so he would be ready to really kick kick kick kick kick it in over the last hundred

Haven't you too chased a toddler down the straightaway of his first race, a cool fifty meters, knowing full well how you sound repeating the absurd instruction to "Stay in your lane!"

Haven't you known a child to physically shake with anticipation before a race. And have you not felt even at a spectator's distance his shaking deep within yourself, as if his body and your body were one body and the body was called life.

Have you not looked at the mid-race picture of the boy suspended midair like some ballerino of the pavement, have you not looked at the picture and felt yourself lift two inches above the ground.

Have you not taken a hundred laps around the living room and then, wanting so very much to keep up, taken a hundred more.

Has that part of you that wishes to protect itself from judgment yet been burned off by the effort. Have you yet run yourself into submission.

Have you not day after day seen what you've never seen before, the child running faster and then faster, farther and then farther, stumbling and then righting.

Have you not been all of these things first.

Have you the courage to express the truth the way a child runs.

Last Night

I dreamed that I was racing five kilometers on the track and was running minutes faster than I'd ever run before when on the penultimate lap I sensed an opportunity and surged past the leader and opened a small gap between us before he made his own move on the homestretch of the last lap and was gaining on me from the outside and likely would have passed me but for the fact that suddenly there were two of me, the one watching from third position as the competitor passed me for second but could not catch the other me, who held him off and claimed victory for all true victors while I looked on proud that at least one of me had won but aware in some quiet part of myself that he was he and I was I.

Ten Miles or So from Home

Starting out on the old familiar trail through the countryside, I see the mountains ahead of me, beneath them the sloping foothills greening in the early summer.

I intend to run north, then west. Home is that way, approximately. In the western distance, rainstorms. I'm where I want to be: on my feet, moving, enjoying the landscape and the way my mind stretches over it.

The ground is thick with mud from the last of the melting snow. I have no choice but to go slowly, so, slowly, I go, slipping occasionally and hoping not to fall. If only I could grow a tail like Chuang Tzu's and drag it through this mud.

If only I could? Perhaps I can.

at home in the mud
here I am and nowhere else
running my own pace

After all, I belong on this path that is mine alone. I belong to this life or to nothing at all. Where does the trail lead? I can't know until I run it. When I do it will take me where only I can go. Were there a thousand of me, each of us would follow the path to our own destination.

I have run this way before, but the trail was not the trail and I was not I. Every day is new.

Turning a bend, I startle a doe, which startles me. Did she fear me a cougar? I look over one shoulder, then the other.

no cougar there
and no cougar there—
no-cougars everywhere

Every so often another runner comes along, or someone on a mountain bike. We nod. One of us steps to the side, making room on the single-track trail for the other to pass. They are going their way, I am going mine.

sometimes I feel
like I have wasted my life
sometimes I don't

I take my time on this journey to the north. This is where I have wanted to be, where I have spent all week looking forward to running. There is no need to race through it now that I am here. It is possible to assume the perspective of stillness.

not moving an inch
in the Gallatin Valley
the world comes to me

The trail is long and winding, gently following the curves of the terrain. I let myself be gentle, too, accepting that the ground will determine my route. I feel small here, almost nonexistent, barely there at the center of experience.

It is as if I have stepped outside of myself and am looking back to see my small figure moving patiently through a vast expanse of geography and time. There I go: back and forth down the switchbacks into the ravine and back and forth up the other side.

> nothing to say
> in the blowing wind—
> running does running

The emptiness here welcomes me. I can see that the storm to the west is bigger now, coming closer. Part of me hopes I will still be running when it arrives, part of me already knows I will be.

Reaching the end of my northerly stretch, I turn to the west and meet a headwind of human presence. Speeding cars, traffic lights, the stink of road-kill skunk, knees suddenly threatening to stiffen up as I pound the concrete.

My thoughts turn to home, where I imagine my wife and our boys going about their days mindless of me and my travails. This happy image goes both ways: it means it is still possible to be on my own. They'll see me when they see me, in due time.

Crossing the university campus, which somehow looks more alive to me on this empty Saturday than it does during the busy week, the rain slowly begins. I spend most of my days on this campus, but only today is it mine.

What is knowledge, I wonder, and what has it to do with running or rain? Not much, I suppose—but truth may be another story.

I am wet now in the blustering wind, ready for anything, even a crosswalk, where I stop to wait for the light to change and receive the shouts of passersby who have opinions about my pink shorts.

Their perspective is irrelevant to me. I have my own perspective: this moment, too, is holy. If they were asking, I would tell them.

Ah, maybe they were asking.

The rain is hard. In moments like this I feel like I could run forever and never die. Only then, if I were lucky, would I notice where I was, past the hubs of commerce, at the edge of a small lake, studying the shore.

no turtles today
reminiscent of cougars
never seen

I could stay here a long time under the cover of a tree watching raindrops collide with the water and listening to their myriad tiny splashes.

small lake
no turtle jumps in—
the sound of water

I could stay here a long time, but the last stretch of my run follows a gravel road, and something about this life feels like a song telling me to continue.